JIM

a.k.a.

the

WONDER

DOG

NANCY B. DAILEY

JIM a.k.a THE WONDER DOG
Copyright © 2018 Nancy B. Dailey
All cover art copyright © 2018
All Rights Reserved

This is a biographical novel based on the real life of Jim The Wonder Dog.

No part of this book may be reproduced or transmitted in any form or by any means, electronic or mechanical, including photocopying, recording, or by any information storage and retrieval system, without permission in writing from the author.

Cover art and drawings by Nancy Dailey

Paperback-Press
an imprint of A & S Publishing
A & S Holmes, Inc.

ISBN-13: 978-1-945669-53-8

DEDICATION

To my friend, Ann Gouge,
whose grandfather
was Jim's vet.

ACKNOWLEDGMENTS

Thank you to all the businesses and organizations that have archived copies of newspapers from cities and towns large and small. Thanks also to the Missouri Historical Society, and Jim the Wonder Dog Memorial Park and Museum for their help

Thank you to the members of the Springfield Writers Workshop, as well as other individuals, for the helpful suggestions and critique.

Thank you Ripley's Believe It Or Not for permission to use their cartoon of Jim, and to Larry Arrowood for permission to use the photos of Pearl Van Arsdale with Jim, and Sam Van Arsdale with Jim.

Thank you to Jim McCarty of the online www.ruralmissouri.coop magazine, who so willingly shared not only the full article he wrote, but also all of his notes, and other items.

And finally, a thank you goes to that nameless librarian at Missouri Valley College who, oh so many years ago, banned the 1942 book by Clarence Dewey Mitchell from the shelves of the college library. Mitchell wrote the book JIM THE WONDER DOG from the dog's point of view. This caused it to be banned with the explanation "dogs cannot talk." By banning that book she definitely sparked my curiosity.

TABLE OF CONTENTS

Dedication iv
Acknowledgments i
Table of Contents ii
Map iii
Chapter 1 – 1925 1
   An Unexpected Delivery 1
Chapter 2 7
   Jim Goes for Training 7
Chapter 3 – 1928 11
   A New Home in Sedalia 11
Chapter 4 – 1931 17
   Jim Goes to the University 17
Chapter 5 23
   In and Around Sedalia 23
   And an Operation for Jim 23
Chapter 6 – 1933 31
   Winter in Florida 31
Chapter 7 – 1933 - 1935 35
   Traveling Continues 35
Chapter 8 – 1936 - 1937 41
   Move to Marshall 41
Chapter 9 – 1937 51
   A Sad Day 51
   Jim Remembered 51
How Did Jim Do It? 55
Questions 59
Photos 61
SOURCES 67
About the Author 91

MAP

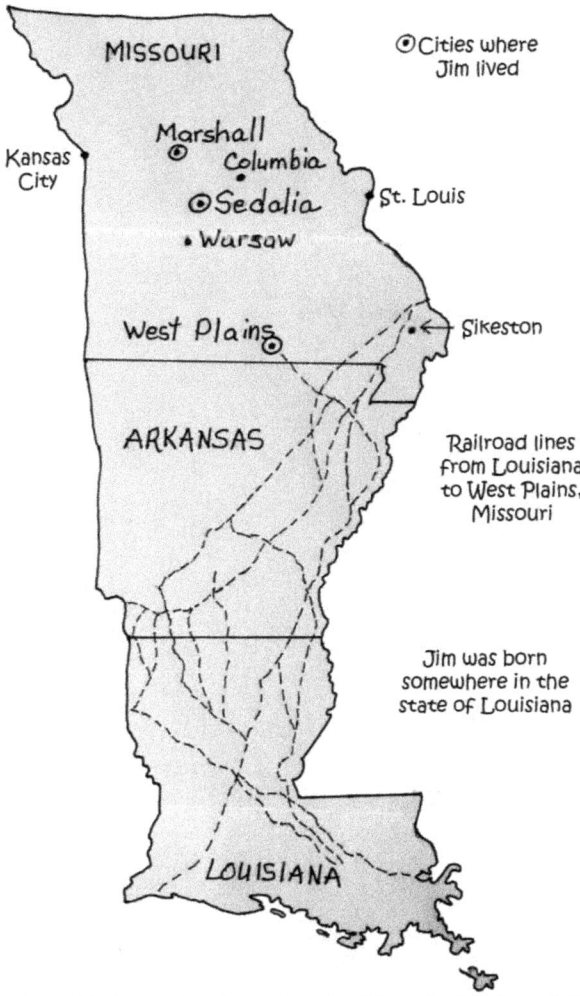

Railroad information based on the Historical Atlas of the North American Railroad by Derek Hayes.

CHAPTER 1 – 1925

An Unexpected Delivery

A railroad express delivery man set the wooden crate on the lobby floor.

"What's this?" asked Sam Van Arsdale, the manager of the hotel.

"Looks like a puppy, Sir," said the delivery man with a grin.

"I didn't order a dog." Sam tilted his head towards the crate. "Take it back."

The deliveryman pointed to the papers attached to the crate. "He came in on today's train, and my job is to deliver him to Mr. Sam Van Arsdale at the Arcade Hotel, West Plains, Missouri. That's you, and I have delivered him. My job is done."

"But...."

"Enjoy your new pup," the man said as he went out the door.

Sam stared at the little black and white puppy in the crate. The puppy stared back.

Some of the guests in the lobby gathered around to see this unexpected delivery.

"Where's he from?"

Sam pulled the papers off the side of the crate and began to read. The six-week-old puppy came from a kennel in Louisiana. He was a purebred Llewellin Setter, a hunting dog from champion stock, a gift from Mr. Taylor. Mr. Taylor? Who was Mr. Taylor?

Meanwhile some of the guests commented on the large paws and unusually large eyes of the pup.

Sam lifted the crate and headed outside. It was time to let the puppy out. He set the crate down on the grassy yard in back of the hotel, and unhooked the door. He reached in, lifted the puppy out and placed him on the grass. Sam noticed again the large paws and unusually large brown eyes.

The puppy wandered around a bit, then returned to Sam and sat down.

"What am I going to do with you?" Sam said. "You're too young to hunt. You're too young to train."

The puppy looked very serious, almost as if he

understood every word. Sam frowned slightly, then abruptly shook his head. "Nah."

Sam's eight-year-old niece, Dorothy Martin, came running out.

"Do you really have a new puppy, Uncle Sam? Can I see him? Ooooh, there he is." She ran over and scooped the puppy up into her arms.

Sam's eyes lit up. Here was a solution...if Dorothy's parents would agree. He told Dorothy to watch the puppy, and went back into the hotel to talk with them. They both nodded their heads, and Sam went back outside.

"Hey, Dorothy," he called. She looked up. "How would you like to keep the puppy for me for awhile?"

"Oh, yes!" She lifted the puppy up and stared into his eyes. "You get to come live with me," she said, "for awhile, anyway."

Dorothy and the puppy had a great time together. She threw a stick, sometimes a rag doll, and the puppy would go after it and bring it back to her. They also played hide and seek. Dorothy told the puppy to stay while she hid. He sat and waited for her to call for him to find her, then he ran straight to wherever she had hidden.

One day Dorothy invented a new game. She placed a cardboard box over the puppy and told him to stay. She then hid a doll, while the puppy waited patiently under the box. When Dorothy returned and removed the box she told him to find the doll. He went right to it. Every single time.

"When I hide the doll, the puppy never has to hunt for it," she told her mother. "He knows where it is and goes right to it."

But her mother didn't believe that nonsense.

One Saturday, during the time the puppy was with Dorothy, Sam and his wife, Pearl, went to the movies. Will Rogers had a role in that movie, and in one scene he went into a cafe for a cup of coffee. The waitress said, "Would you mind telling me who you are?" Will Rogers replied, "I have no name, lady. You can just call me Jim."

Later Sam and Pearl decided to see how the puppy was getting along.

"The puppy's really smart!" said Dorothy. "He knows what I tell him. When I tell him to stay while I go hide, and then I call him, he finds me right away. He doesn't even have to hunt."

"That's because he is a hunting dog," said Sam. "He has a good nose and good retrieving instincts."

"But I also tell him to stay while I go hide my dolly," she said. "And when I come back and tell him to find my dolly, he goes right to where I hid her. He doesn't have to hunt, Uncle Sam, he just knows where she is."

Sam remained unconvinced.

He looked down at the puppy sitting next to Dorothy. The big-footed pup with the large eyes and no name sat staring at Sam. No name. That scene from the movie popped into Sam's head. "Well," he said, "guess I'll call you Jim."

CHAPTER 2

Jim Goes for Training

When Jim was old enough to be trained to hunt birds, Sam took him to Ira Irvine, a well-known dog trainer with kennels about eight miles north of West Plains.

Ira asked Sam where he got the dog. Sam related the story of the pup he had not ordered, and had certainly not expected, being delivered to him. But Sam also remembered something else. He remembered previously chatting with a traveling salesman from Louisiana. He had mentioned to the salesman that he was looking for a good pup to train for bird season coming up that fall. The salesman then talked up his fine litter of puppies. Why, they came from champions, the best hunting dogs ever, he said. Sam laughed and called him a braggart. The salesman offered to sell one of the puppies for the price of $25, a huge amount at that time. Sam quickly declined; the salesman laughed and called Sam a miser. That salesman must have been Mr. Taylor.

Neither Ira nor Sam could figure out why Mr. Taylor had just given away what must be an expensive dog.

Jim did not do what Ira told him to do. The other dogs first learned to run zig-zag back and forth across the field, searching for the smell of birds. As soon as they picked up the scent, they learned to go on point by standing still, heads held high and tails straight, facing the direction where the birds were hidden. Next they had to get used to the nearby sound of gunshot, and finally they learned to retrieve the dead bird, bringing it back without chewing or puncturing it.

Jim just watched.

During those hot summer days of training, Jim stayed in the shade. Ira absolutely could not get Jim to join in those lessons. He was as perplexed as anyone could be.

"Lazy dog."

Maybe that was why Mr. Taylor had given him away.

Sam returned to find out how well Jim did, or in this case, didn't do.

But Ira was not yet ready to give up on Jim. "There's something special about this big-footed, lazy dog, Sam. Look at those eyes! They look intelligent...and almost human."

Sam agreed to leave him with Ira awhile longer. Might as well; he couldn't send the pup back to where it had come from.

In early November Sam went back to check on his uncooperative dog.

Ira didn't say much, he just took Sam and Jim out to hunt. It was the first time Jim had been taken out alone without other dogs around. When they got out of the car, Jim went about twenty feet and locked on point. Sam and Ira walked up and flushed the birds. The quail exploded upward in a whirring flurry of feathers, spreading out across the far end of the area. Jim went straight to one bird and pointed. When the bird flew, Sam shot. "Dead bird," he said. Jim moved forward, found the bird and brought it back.

This scene was repeated many times that day. Each time Jim went straight to where the birds were. None of this zig-zag stuff for him!

"Smart dog," Sam said. Apparently Ira had managed to train the dog after all.

Ira agreed the dog was smart, but admitted that Jim hadn't needed any training. "He seems to know exactly where the birds are. Never seen anything like it," he said.

Jim soon became known in the area as an excellent bird dog. Sam apparently kept a running count of the number of quail shot while hunting with him, but quit counting at 5,000. That was more than any other hunting dog in history.

But Jim had only just begun to show his talents.

CHAPTER 3 – 1928

A New Home in Sedalia

The explosion was heard for three miles. The dance hall floor blew up and then fell back down into the fire. This was April 13, 1928. Three other buildings were damaged. Of those three, the Arcade Hotel suffered the worst.

Sam Van Arsdale found another hotel to manage. He, Pearl, and Jim, moved into the LaMoore Hotel in Sedalia.

One hot day while out hunting, Sam decided to take a break. "Let's go sit under the hickory tree," he said. Jim went right to a hickory tree and sat down. Really? Did Jim actually know that was a hickory tree? Or was it only a coincidence?

"Show me a black oak tree," said Sam. Jim walked to a black oak tree. Then, on command, Jim went to a walnut tree, a cedar tree, even a stump.

Back home, Sam excitedly told his wife of Jim's amazing abilities to distinguish types of trees. Pearl didn't believe it. She did agree, though, to go back with them to see for herself. Once again Jim went directly to each tree he was asked to find. There were no mistakes. Pearl was speechless. She was also concerned, and asked Sam not to tell anybody else.

But this was a discovery Sam just could not keep secret.

At first he told friends he saw in town while he was out walking Jim. But he could tell by the tone of their voices and the looks on their faces that they didn't believe him.

However, somebody must have asked the right question, maybe something like: If Jim can pick out a specific tree, can he pick out my car? Can he find a Dodge? A Chevrolet? The doctor's car? All of which Jim did, plus more.

That got people's attention.

Soon Jim regularly performed in the lobby of the hotel. The lobby was a gathering place for guests to relax and visit. No one had a TV in their room or in their houses. There were no electronic games, no cell phones. So people got together and talked. And Sam was usually ready to show them Jim's abilities.

"Where is the man here with a brown mustache?" Jim went to him.

"Show us a lady wearing a blue dress." Jim went to her.

"There's a man here who is a traveling salesman. Can you show us who that is?" Jim walked over and put his paw on a man wearing a suit. Yes, he was a traveling salesman.

The LaMoore Hotel where the Van Arsdales and Jim lived had a dining room accessible through a small gate in the lobby. Sam told Jim never to go through that gate into the dining room because some guests wouldn't like that. Jim never did. When Sam went into the dining room Jim would lie down in the corner of the lobby and wait.

Sam took Jim with him when he visited other places. One warm summer afternoon they drove to the little town of Warsaw, Missouri.

Very quickly a crowd gathered as the word spread that Sam and Jim were in town. For the next hour Jim showed off his remarkable abilities. Nobody could figure out how he did it.

"What would I do if I had a stomachache?" Sam asked.

Jim wagged his tail and trotted over to Dr.

Savage. He nudged the doctor. This was Jim's first time in this town and he couldn't know who the doctor was. Could he?

"What made Henry Ford rich?" The dog walked over and looked at a car—a Ford.

"See if you can find a car with the license plate number 132875." Jim crossed the street, and placed his paws on the running board of a car. It was the county tax collector's car; the license plate number was 132875.

Someone in the crowd said something in French. Sam did not understand, but Jim did. When Sam asked him to do what the man said, Jim wove his way among the legs of the people in the crowd until he reached the back. There he looked at one gentleman, sat down in front of him, and raised his paw, touching the man's knee. Turned out the man was a minister. Sam asked the man who had spoken in French, "What did you say?"

"I asked if there was a Bible in the crowd."

The minister then reached in his inside coat pocket and brought out a small New Testament.

Almost every day Sam Van Arsdale went to buy a cigar. Of course, Jim went along. Sam would say, "Jim, show the man what cigar I smoke." And Jim would put his paw on the glass case in front of the Chancellor cigars.

But one day the clerk had rearranged the

placement of the cigars, probably to see how the dog would react. Sam asked Jim to show the man which cigar he smoked. Jim immediately went to the other end of the case and put his paw where the Chancellor cigars had been moved. Couldn't fool him.

Sam and Pearl went on a vacation to the North Woods of upper Minnesota in the summer of 1931. One day Sam and another man went to some small lakes to get bait and then do some fishing. Jim went with them. The water was shallow at the edge of the first lake, and hundreds of little frogs constantly jumped around on the bank. Apparently Jim was intrigued because he stayed behind and watched them all morning. When the men returned, Jim was still walking in the shallow water towards the frogs, which made them jump. Later, back at the cabin Sam told Pearl about Jim's fascination with the frogs. He then casually asked Jim what the frogs did. Jim hopped in an odd way from a sitting position with his front legs held stiff.

This was the only trick Jim ever did.

"He despises trick stuff," Sam told people when they asked if Jim could do any of the normal dog tricks. No, he wouldn't do any of them; he sulked when Sam tried to teach him. As for jumping around like a frog when Sam told him to, well, "He thought of that himself."

CHAPTER 4 – 1931

Jim Goes to the University

Sam Van Arsdale, along with everybody else, wanted to know how Jim did all those things, how he knew what to do. So Sam arranged for a meeting with two professors at the University of Missouri to see if they could determine what might explain Jim's abilities.

According to a newspaper article in the Sedalia Democrat (Thursday, Dec. 3, 1931) Jim was to be given an intelligence test. Not only that, but the Paramount Film Company would also film the test with the idea of making a sound picture at a later date featuring Jim. Many movies were still silent at this time.

The following day Sam and Jim traveled to the university campus in Columbia. Dr. A. J. Durant, professor of Veterinary Science, was in charge. Dr. Sherman Dickinson, professor of the College of Agriculture, assisted. Both worked with animals and had a lot of experience.

They both examined six-year-old Jim. They agreed that Jim was physically the same as a dog of ordinary intelligence except that his eyes were more readily noticeable, and the middle portion of his cranium was very broad.

Then, they all moved to the quadrangle— something like a courtyard— in back of Jesse Hall. Several hundred students and faculty members gathered in front of the six columns, all that was left of the first building on campus after a fire in 1892. Psychologists from both Missouri University and Washington University in St. Louis were also in the crowd to see what Jim would do.

J. J. Herrmann, a cameraman for Paramount Motion Pictures, took several hundred feet of film of Jim at work. Paramount News, a division of the motion picture company, produced newsreels which were shown twice a week in movie theaters across the U.S. The footage of Jim's performance was sent to New York to be made into either a picture reel, or as part of a news reel to be shown in theaters within a few weeks.

To start the demonstration, which was also a test for Jim, Sam told the dog to go find the man who takes care of animals. Jim walked over to Dr. Durant and put his paw on the veterinarian's leg. "Where is Professor Dickinson?" Sam asked. Jim walked over to him.

Then came requests in various languages. In Italian, Jim was asked to show an elm tree. Jim walked over to an elm tree and put his paw on the trunk. In French, he was asked to show the car with a specific license number. He did. Jim was asked in German to point out a girl dressed in blue. He did that, too. And in Spanish he was asked to show them a man with a black mustache. Jim went to a man with a small black Charlie Chaplin type mustache. (This small mustache just over the center of the upper lip was made popular by the silent screen actor Charlie Chaplin, before movies had sound. It later lost its popularity because of its association with Adolf Hitler in World War II.)

"There is a person in the crowd with a nose for news," said Sam. "Who is he?"

Jim went straight to a reporter.

When it was suggested that Jim point out a young man who had recently had his hair permed, though, Jim was unable to do that. As soon as that request was made, a young man in the crowd quickly turned and ran away. Apparently that was the boy with the new perm.

There was also a bit of humor in the crowd that day. Someone said that Dr. Walter Williams (the president of the university) should give an honorary degree to this dog with "horse sense." Someone else shouted out that at last intelligence had been shown on the campus.

At the end of Jim's demonstration Dr. Dickinson concluded that Jim was the smartest dog he had ever seen, that he had detected no signals from Mr. Van Arsdale, there had been nothing to guide the dog. Dr. Durant was convinced that Jim possessed an unknown ability that might never come again to a dog for many, many generations.

Unfortunately for movie goers, the news feature on Jim was never made. The reason given by Paramount, printed in the Wausau Daily Herald in Wisconsin on March 4, 1932, stated that, "You can't screen an intelligent dog like you can a stunt dog." The LaPlata Home Press of LaPlata, Missouri, on October 6, 1932, agreed, saying that while you can film trick dogs, "you can't film a brilliant dog." It also quoted one of the film makers saying, "the picture just didn't look reasonable," and that "the performance had not been presented in a way to be convincing."

Well, that was disappointing.

Later Sam received an extremely generous

offer of money with a contract to have Jim work in movies for a year. Sam turned it down, saying that he and Jim could not hunt in Hollywood. Makes sense to people and dogs who go hunting every chance they get.

There were also offers for Jim to star in dog food commercials. Sam turned them all down.

While commercial dog food was gaining acceptance, there were only two choices: Ken-L-Ration, which was canned horse meat, and Milkbone dog biscuits. Most folks still fed their dogs table scraps. Jim was also fed table scraps, perhaps better quality than what other dogs were fed. His favorite food was cornbread.

CHAPTER 5

In and Around Sedalia

And an Operation for Jim

Almost every day Jim entertained a crowd of people.

One morning, a barber telephoned Sam Van Arsdale and asked him to bring some tied fishing flies, an artificial type of lure, often handmade, to the barber shop. Jim, as usual, went with Sam, and when they arrived there were already several people there. Sam immediately asked Jim which man had requested the flies. Jim walked over and placed his paw on a man, who looked up, astounded.

"How is that possible?"

Sam shrugged. "I have no explanation; I don't know."

Another time they visited the Kemper Military Academy in Boonville, Missouri. The cadets assembled, all dressed alike in their military uniforms.

"Jim, show us the shortest cadet here."

Jim strolled down the perfectly aligned rows of cadets as if inspecting the troops. He stopped. Right in front of the shortest one.

Someone handed Sam a hand-written note. He looked at it, showed the note to Jim, and then said, "Jim, do what this note says." Jim walked over to a red-haired boy, at which point Sam read the note out loud: Have Jim show us a boy who has red hair.

"Jim, who is a person with a title beginning with the letter L?" Jim walked over to a lieutenant.

Then Sam tried something new. He spelled what he wanted Jim to find, instead of saying it. "Show us a cadet who has on g-l-a-s-s-e-s." Jim sauntered over to a cadet wearing glasses and lifted his paw.

One day at a gas station the attendant-owner asked if he could see Jim do something.

Sam turned, looked at Jim and said, "Where does this man keep his money?"

Instead of going to the cash register, Jim went

to a stack of old tires piled in the corner.

"He's right," said the shocked attendant. He then explained that the station had recently been broken into and robbed, and since then he'd hidden the cash among the old tires.

Time for a new hiding place?

Another day Jim performed in front of Hoffman's Hardware Store. At one point Sam said, "Show me the sign spelled H-O-F-F-M-A-N." Jim immediately ran around the corner of the building. Sam followed, saying, "Jim, you didn't listen to me." But when Sam turned the corner he saw Jim with his paw resting on another Hoffman sign. This sign was lower, one that Jim could more easily reach.

Not everyone believed that Jim could really do these things on his own. Usually, though, after watching a performance, they changed their minds. And when a skeptical person still accused Sam of somehow signaling the dog, Sam would say, "Show me how I do it. I'd like to know."

People always gathered when Sam and Jim were out for a walk. They often strolled down Ohio Street in the main business area of Sedalia. And occasionally a reporter from the Kansas City Times would also be in town, often wanting to hear and see more about Jim. On January 25, 1932, Sam shared a story of something that happened in their rooms at the hotel.

"A few days ago we got some pictures of Jim's two pups," Sam said, adding that they were being trained at West Plains. When he asked Pearl where they were, she couldn't remember where she had put them. Jim got up, walked over to the dresser, and put his paw on a dresser drawer; on the right end of the middle drawer. "We opened the drawer, and there they were."

Then Sam looked down at the dog and said, "Now show us how the frogs went, Jim." And Jim immediately did a series of his strange, awkward little hops.

Charles M. Howell of Kansas City was seeking the nomination for the Democratic candidate for U.S. senator. On July 20, 1932, he had lunch with several of his supporters at the La Moore Hotel. Sam Van Arsdale visited with everybody gathered in the lobby, of course. And, of course, he involved Jim.

When asked who the next U.S. senator would be, Jim walked across the lobby and placed his paw on Mr. Howell. Then Jim was asked to find a football player in the crowd. He nudged Mr. Le Mire, who had been a half-back and captain of the Tiger football team at the University of Missouri. Then Sam asked if there was a man in the crowd who had the same name as a Missouri county. Jim again went to Mr. Howell.

Jim became known as "the mystery dog of Sedalia."

In 1932 Sam received an invitation from J. Alex Sloan, in the department of special events, to have a booth for Jim at the World's Fair in Chicago. They made the necessary arrangements for his appearance.

The Van Arsdales, and Jim, of course, visited family in Sikeston, Missouri, quite often. In late September, 1932, during one of those visits, the Sikeston Standard reported that Jim, the educated bird dog and member of the Van Arsdale family, would be located in the Science Building at the World's Fair in Chicago next year.

"That is if Jim lives another year, and if the World's Fair buildings do not slip off into the lake from which ground was stolen to support the buildings." (This new ground for the fair was dredged up from the bottom of Lake Michigan.)

Apparently those Missourians didn't have much faith in reclaimed land being permanent. The fair was spread out over 424 acres, with almost the entire amount of land being filled in along the shore of Lake Michigan between 12th and 39th streets.

On a crisp morning in early November, 1932, Sam, his father-in-law, G. P. Martin, and Jim, left Sedalia and headed south. Their destination was Warsaw, Missouri, 35 miles away. Frost sparkled on the ground—a good day for hunting, even though the fields were a bit muddy. They hunted in one field all morning.

The birds then flew into another field. Jim headed through a wire fence after them, but his right front leg got hung up in the wire. What was worse, was that Jim was caught in a position that left all of his weight on that leg.

When Sam and G. P. caught up, they quickly freed Jim from the wire, and they all went on hunting. They noticed Jim limping, so they decided to let him rest when they came to a spring. Jim lay down in the cold water. After awhile they resumed hunting until both men had twenty birds each. Then they were ready to go home.

What they didn't know at the time was this was Jim's last day to hunt.

Later, at home, Sam noticed that Jim seemed very tired. When called, he slowly got up. His leg was stiff when he limped over to Sam. Jim did not want Sam touching the affected leg. By 9 o'clock that evening Jim was noticeably worse.

Sam called Dr. M. E. Gouge, who came right away to the hotel. Dr. Gouge treated Jim, working with him throughout the night and most of the next day. However, Jim's condition worsened. Finally Dr. Gouge decided to call the esteemed veterinarian, Dr. J. C. Flynn, 85 miles away in Kansas City. He placed the call around 9 p.m.; Dr. Flynn rushed into the LaMoore Hotel in Sedalia at 11:45 that night.

After examining Jim and conferring with Dr. Gouge, the decision was made to place Jim in Dr. Flynn's care at his small animal hospital in Kansas City.

The Van Arsdales and Jim traveled to Kansas City, Missouri, to see Dr. Flynn for Jim's treatment. But first came the x-rays. One x-ray was taken, but when they attempted to change Jim's position to the opposite side, he wanted nothing to do with that. He left the table and eluded capture, but soon returned and placed a paw on the table.

"Just talk to him as you would talk to a person," Sam told the doctor. Dr. Flynn then told Jim what he wanted. Jim got on the table and stretched out with the correct side available for the second x-ray to be taken.

The x-rays showed that Jim needed an operation on his shoulder. He would remain in Dr. Flynn's care for a week.

Dr. Flynn took Jim home with him each night. The first night he told Jim that his baby daughter was in the northwest room upstairs, and asked Jim to go check on her. Jim headed upstairs. When Dr.

Flynn reached his daughter's room, there was Jim with his paw on the cradle.

In the office, if Jim got up on the table and he was facing the wrong way, Dr. Flynn would simply say, "You're turned the wrong way," and Jim would turn around.

Sam called every day to see how Jim was doing. Dr. Flynn quickly noticed that Jim pretty much ignored the telephone. But if the phone rang and Jim got up and went to the phone, it meant that Sam was on the other end.

Two reports of the operation give differing versions. One report said that Jim was operated on for adhesions resulting from rheumatism in the shoulder; the other report said the operation was to remove a tumor in the shoulder. The operation was a success.

CHAPTER 6 – 1933

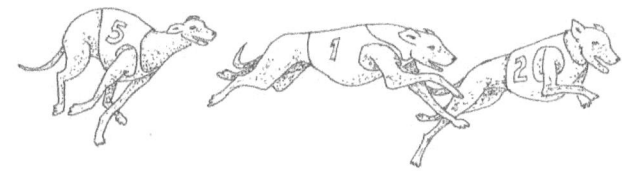

Winter in Florida

Sam, Pearl, and Jim left Sedalia the end of September, 1932, to spend several weeks with Sam's brother. They stayed at the Marshall Hotel in Sikeston, Missouri, which G. P. owned, and where he lived.

In December, Sam and Jim were invited to a Sikeston Chamber of Commerce meeting. J. E. Harper, of the executive committee, could not decide whether to believe in Jim's abilities or not. He had read about them, but wanted to see for himself. Because of that, Sam and Jim were invited to appear at the executive committee meeting on

Friday, December 9th.

When the time came, Sam asked Jim, "Who would you pick out if you wanted some bread?" Jim hobbled over to Emanual Schorle (of the Schorle Brothers Bakery), and tapped him on the knee with his paw.

Jim still suffered from rheumatism and some stiffness in his right front leg. It did not, however, keep him from continuing to amaze people with his performances.

When asked about a man there wearing a r-e-d s-w-e-a-t-e-r, Jim pointed out a man wearing a hunting coat. Guess what? Underneath that coat the man had on a red sweater.

Sam asked Jim to find the gentleman wearing a hat like Al Smith wears, but of a different color. (Al Smith had been governor of New York, and in 1928 a Democratic candidate for President of the U. S. He always wore a brown derby hat, a hat which was round on top.) Jim went to a salesman wearing that same type of hat; this man's derby was black instead of brown.

Danny Malone watched it all, but was still convinced that there was some kind of trick to it. Later when Sam held scraps of paper down so Jim could see what to do instead of being told, Danny thought he had figured out the trick. To prove it to himself, on a piece of paper he wrote, in French, "point out the cigar case." He handed the paper to

Sam who glanced at it, then held it down at dog level.

"You read it, Jim," said Sam. "I can't."

Jim promptly went to the cigar counter and put his paw on the glass case. Danny was astounded. And that's when Danny Malone became a believer.

Mr. and Mrs. Van Arsdale, and Jim, then traveled to Florida for the winter. Their purpose was to help Jim, since the warmth of a Florida winter would be better for his rheumatism than the cold of a Missouri winter. While in Florida they visited Tampa, Miami, and other resorts.

In Miami, they stayed in a hotel near a racetrack where dog races were held. They also visited the Henry Hunt family who were relatives. The family liked to listen to radio broadcasts of the races. Someone asked if Jim could pick the winners. So they clipped from the newspaper the names of the dogs entered in a particular race. Each person held a name. Jim was asked to show who held the first place winner, who had the second place winner, and finally who had the third place winner.

For two days the Hunt children placed bets according to Jim's predictions. They won a lot of money, and a local paper found out what they were doing. Of course they printed this information.

Later, when the Van Arsdales got back to their hotel they found a telegram: "Get that dog out of town or something is going to happen to him."

They packed up and left that night.

While visiting with the S. H. Gillespie family in Tampa, one of them went along to the racetrack in Miami. Jim missed one of the winners. Later they discovered that Jim's pick was "scratched" at the last minute.

Interestingly enough The Tampa Tribune printed a short article on Saturday, February 25, 1933, in which an upset Sam stated that Jim did not pick lottery numbers, and that they were not a part of gambling. Apparently many people were now asking that Jim pick the winners for them in various lotteries.

Back home again in Sedalia, Sam discovered that reports of Jim's ability to pick a racing winner had not died down, but had spread. He received a telegram from a lady in another state asking for Jim to pick the horse that would be the winner of the derby. Sam did not reply; instead he and Jim went fishing.

CHAPTER 7 – 1933 - 1935

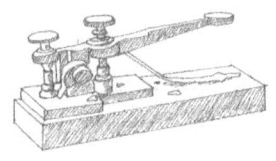

Traveling Continues

"JIM, HIMSELF, ARRIVES FOR VISIT IN CITY" proclaimed the headline of an article on the first page of the Sikeston newspaper, dated April 7, 1933. The Van Arsdales had come to town the previous Wednesday, and Jim had already given a performance. He was also scheduled to meet with a group of grade school and high school students while he was in town.

Skeptics do not remain skeptics when they see Jim, said another article in the same paper. Everyone who was a critic, and everyone who did not believe becomes "another booster for Jim."

The adage "seeing is believing"—still true.

Towards the end of May they were back again in Sikeston after spending several weeks fishing in Arkansas.

Jim was scheduled to appear at the World's Fair in Chicago starting on Thursday, June 1, 1933, but that did not happen. Since he still suffered with rheumatism, Sam decided it might be too much for Jim.

Jim performed for a number of various organizations. One of those was the Fish, Game, and Forest League of Missouri. That group held their January meeting in Kansas City, at the Cocked Hat, located on 45th Street and Troost Avenue. The meeting featured a demonstration by—as they put it, "S. H. Van Arsdale's Jim, the educated dog."

Throughout their travels, Sam and Pearl would not stay at any hotel that would not allow Jim to stay in the room also. Usually, though, permission was granted after the owner or manager watched Jim perform. The consensus seemed to be that since Jim was not an ordinary dog, he could stay.

On Valentine's Day in 1935, Jim "amazed" crowds "with feats that border on miraculous" in Moberly, Missouri, at the Merchants Hotel. Although Jim was noticeably tired and probably would have rather been left alone, he continued to do what Sam asked. The Moberly newspaper described Jim as the "epitome of culture and social graces." The article said Jim was courteous, never walked in front of anyone, and would go around behind Sam's chair to stretch out.

"Jim" Van Arsdale was invited to give a public appearance for a joint session of the Missouri state legislature in Jefferson City. That took place on Wednesday, April 24, 1935, at 2:30 in the afternoon. Governor Guy Park was also in attendance to watch the performance.

Sam and Jim were introduced by Representative Jack Jolly of Pettis County, the county in which Jim and the Van Arsdales lived. The General Assembly interrupted its debate on the sales tax to watch this now famous dog.

Among the things Jim was asked to do was to show where there was some foliage in the room. He went to a palm tree growing in a large ceramic pot. He was asked to point out a gentleman whom the ladies thought was tall and handsome. He walked over to Morris Osborn, a legislator known for his style and good looks.

Outside, Jim identified cars by their license numbers, and/or the type of car. Then Mr. W. D. Meng said he's like to see if Jim could point out the car in which he came.

But Sam first told Jim to find a car from Nebraska. Jim walked a short distance to the left of where the two stood, and pointed out a car with

Nebraska license plates.

"Now do what Mr. Meng requires of you," said Sam.

Jim turned and walked to the right, past the two men, on down the street a ways and stopped in front of a DeSoto. It was the correct car.

Back inside, a telegrapher tapped out a message in Morse Code using a telegraph key. It took training for someone to be able to send a message in code, as well as to decipher it. Morse Code was "written" as a sequence of dots and dashes. The length of a dot was the basic unit; the length of a dash was three times that of a dot. Various sequences of dots and dashes made up the twenty-six letters of the alphabet. Normally a telegraph message was sent long distance over wires using electrical signals called dits and dahs, probably for the sounds they made as they were being tapped out.

Jim listened to the dits and dahs, then walked to a Senator sitting in the back and placed a paw on that gentleman. Sam had not been told the question being asked, so he could only tell Jim to do what the message asked him to do. The telegrapher had asked Jim to find the person who sponsored the Race Horse law…and he did.

On a visit to West Plains, Missouri, at one of Jim's performances was a very skeptical young lady who just remained unconvinced. After awhile Sam looked at Jim and said," There's someone here who thinks you're a fake. What do you think of her?" Jim walked up to the woman and gave a low growl. The crowd thought that was pretty funny.

In October of 1934 Jim gained a new name: "that wonderful Van Arsdale fish hound."

In a conversation with John W. Stoner, the district manager for Southwestern Bell Telephone Company, Sam told Mr. Stoner about fishing at the Lake of the Ozarks. He was in the boat, along with Jim, looking for a good spot…and Jim "pointed." It was a good place to fish, and Sam told Mr. Stoner where it was.

Mr. Stoner found that spot and caught a large seven pound jack salmon.

Under general news in the Kemmerer, Wyoming, newspaper of August 30, the state game and fish commissioner reported that the sage chicken hunting season had just closed, with these birds having been especially plentiful. Sam would have enjoyed the hunt.

Interestingly…in another section of that same paper a headline stated: Wonder Dog Was Here Wednesday.

The article, written by the Gazette's editor, C. Watt Brandon, stated that Jim, "who sees all and knows all," was in Kemmerer Wednesday evening. and those who had not seen the exhibition would not believe what this dog could do.

Brandon reported that Ivan S. Jones walked into the lobby of the Kemmer Hotel where he, Jim, and Sam were. On a piece of paper someone wrote, asking who the prosecuting attorney of the county was. Sam showed the paper to Jim, who looked at it, then walked over and put his paw on Mr. Jones' knee. Mr Jones was, indeed, the county prosecuting attorney.

After describing some more of Jim's feats, the editor said that the exhibition Jim put on was impressive enough to make anyone believe.

(In an online version of the Kemmerer Gazette, an article posted September 2, 2010, stated that their original article about Jim, printed in 1935, was the first to refer to Jim as "the wonder dog." However, there are at least ten Missouri newspaper articles and one Florida newspaper article that used "wonder dog" in the body of their articles or in their headlines, from 1931 to April, 1935. That's a period of from four years to four months before the Kemmerer, Wyoming, article appeared.)

CHAPTER 8 – 1936 - 1937

Move to Marshall

The Van Arsdales and Jim moved to Marshall, Missouri, in February 1936, to run the Ruff Hotel located just off the square in downtown. This may not have been their first move to Marshall; there are indications that they may have been there before. Either way, a lot happened while they lived there, but precious little was ever recorded in the Marshall newspapers. Most of what is known about this period of Jim's life is from the memories of people who lived in the area.

"Everyone around town knew Jim," said Mary Pemberton. "We more or less accepted him as being something unusual and went on with things."

Or, as John Adams said, "We were so used to the dog that we didn't think about how amazing it was."

Many years later, some of the residents in and around Marshall came together to record their memories of Jim on a DVD.

Harold Lickey remembered the time he, his wife, and friends finished dinner at the Ruff Hotel, and they asked if Sam would demonstrate Jim's talents. Sam called Jim over, and asked, "Jim, is anyone here carrying a white purse?" Jim walked over and put his paw on Harold's wife's knee. Yes, she had a white purse. Jim pointed out various people with certain colored clothes, and then showed them a traveling salesman who was headed for Chicago in the morning.

Mary Burge told of another incident with a purse. She was five years old when she first met Jim. She had some pennies in her purse that she planned on spending later. But Sam told Jim to "bring me the purse of someone that has ten pennies in it." Jim went over to Mary, put the strap of her purse in his mouth, and carried it off to Sam." Mary burst out crying.

"What's wrong, honey?" asked Sam.

"He has my ten cents," she sobbed. "I was going to buy twenty pieces of candy."

Sam immediately had Jim return the purse,

which he did, holding it up to Mary so she could reach it.

Mary also related a totally different type of incident she experienced with Jim. One time when her family was downtown, Mary and her brother, Kirby, were playing outside the stores while their parents shopped inside. When her parents were ready to leave, they didn't see the children and didn't know where they were. According to Mary, Sam heard them say this, so he looked at Jim and said, "Jim, there is a girl and boy whose parents are waiting for them. Would you get them?" Jim headed outside, found them, and herded them back to their parents.

A beautiful, large, full-size portrait of Jim hung in the lobby, just above the hotel register. Pearl Van Arsdale was the artist. It took her three weeks to complete the painting; Jim posed thirty minutes each day while Pearl painted. Standing still for that long at a time is no small feat…at least for most dogs! He was the perfect model.

Again, those who saw the painting commented about how striking Jim's eyes were.

On Wednesday, March 11, 1936, the Southwestern Greyhound bus lines began operating through Marshall. The first bus to arrive was at 6 a.m., with others throughout the day. The Ruff

Hotel would now include a ticket office and waiting room for the buses. The stopping place for the Greyhound buses was in front of the hotel coffee shop.

The hotel was very busy. Various groups of people and businesses held meetings there, and had lunch in the dining room. Traveling salesmen relaxed on the couches. Those same salesmen, and hundreds of newspaper stories about Jim, made even more people aware of this special dog and his abilities. Sam also had a picture of Jim put on a billboard out on the highway, directing visitors to the Ruff Hotel. Tourists often crowded the entrance of the hotel just for a peek at Jim. And local people who liked being part of that atmosphere often came simply to "hang out."

Al Boos reported that Jim helped Sam with the hotel business. When someone checked in, if Sam told Jim their room number he would lead the way to the correct room. Jim was even more helpful, though, when someone handed Sam a check, If Jim backed up it meant the check was no good; Sam would not accept the check. But one time a man was so persuasive that even though Jim backed up, Sam took the check anyway. It bounced. Score another one for Jim.

Roy Reade, who ran the barber shop across from the Ruff Hotel, would sometimes go the hotel if he had no customers. According to Roy, Jim spent most of the time napping next to the front desk where Sam worked. "But there'd always be someone wanting that dog to do something. Sam would call to Jim and the dog would get up, do what he was asked and flop back down again. A lot of times that dog acted like he was disgusted."

Birdie Lee McAlister, the daughter of a dentist, talked about the time, as a child, she went with three other people to visit the Van Arsdales. After she, her mother, an aunt, and a cousin were seated, Sam asked Jim which person was the dentist's wife. "The dog came over and put his foot right on Mother's lap," she said.

Birdie remembered another visit, this one on a hot summer day. Everyone complained about the heat. Pearl said something about a bath for Jim so he could cool off. After awhile they noticed that the dog was no longer in the lobby with them. Pearl went upstairs to check. "Sure enough," she said, "Jim was sitting in the bathtub waiting for someone to turn the water on."

She also remembered that Pearl kept fancy pillows on the bed. But when Sam took a nap, he would toss them on the floor. Pearl didn't like that and got onto Sam several times. One time after Sam got up from a nap, Pearl went to the bedroom and found Jim putting the fancy pillows back on the bed.

Another story Birdie related was when the Van

Arsdales were getting ready to leave on a trip. Pearl was finishing packing; Sam had gone to the barber. Pearl heard their car horn honking and thought Sam was telling her to hurry up. Sam heard the horn and thought Pearl was telling him to hurry up. When they got to the car, there was Jim in the driver's seat, honking the horn.

John W. Adams went to a neighbor's house to play bridge. The Van Arsdales and Jim were also there. Sam asked Jim to find the man with the red necktie. "The dog came right over to me and placed his paw on my knee," said John. He thought that was doubly amazing because dogs were supposed to be color blind.

Charles Fitzgerald, who did a lot of electrical work for the hotel, told about watching Jim do something unusual. Several salesmen were sitting around, telling stories as usual. Then Sam asked Jim which man had the most change in his pocket. There was no way Sam could know this, but Jim did. The men emptied their pockets and started counting. Before they were finished Jim sat in front of the right one.

Charles Bradford remembered back when he was twenty he spent a lot of time playing pool at the hotel. All he remembered about the dog was "a lazy lookin' setter just lay there."

Billy Ray Moore said when he was about ten-years-old he remembered that after going to the movies they would buy sugar cookies and go to the hotel. If Sam were not there, they would feed Jim the cookies.

Jim Gabb was a skeptic. He thought that if the dog stopped at a certain car, it was because something was smeared on that car and Jim smelled it. That was why he stopped and put his paw on that car. That might have worked for choosing only one car, but when Jim picked out various cars? Mr. Gabb was not convinced until the day Sam told Jim to pick out the person wearing brown and white shoes. Most people wore solid color shoes. Jim went straight to Mr. Gabb and planted a paw right on one of his brown and white shoes.

Della Mae Soloman remembered waiting in the hotel lobby for a bus. She noticed that Sam stood behind a counter and another man was in front. Then the man looked at her and said, "Lady would you take that note out of the dog's mouth?" She looked down to see Jim sitting in front of her with a piece of paper in his mouth. As she reached for it, the man asked her to read out loud what the note said. "Take this to the lady with a red hat on," she read. "I was flabbergasted!" said Della Mae. "The man was, too."

Jim was also good at something else—he could out stare anybody! He'd win a staring contest every time. As Earl Shannon said, "It was impossible to look him in the eye, he'd look holes through you.

He could stare you down."

In 1936, Jim predicted that the Yankees would win the World Series. Before the seven baseball games were played, Sam and his friends gathered to listen to the broadcast of the first game on the radio. Sam placed two slips of paper in front of the dog. "Jim, I have here the names of the two teams playing in the World Series. Will you show us the one that will win?" One paper had the name "Yankees" on it, the other paper had "Giants."

Jim placed a paw on "Yankees." The Yankees won six of the seven games to become the champions.

He also predicted that Franklin D. Roosevelt would be re-elected president. The names Roosevelt and Landon were printed on two pieces of paper and placed in a hat. Mrs. Ira Irvine and Mrs. Martin each drew out one of the names.

When asked which person was holding the name of the next president, Jim went to Mrs. Martin. She held the name "Roosevelt."

They tried it again to see if Jim would pick the same name. This time he went to Mrs. Irvine. The name she held? Roosevelt.

On the first Saturday in May every year, the Kentucky Derby was held in Louisville, Kentucky. Each year for seven years the names of each horse entered were written on slips of paper and placed on the floor. Jim was asked to choose the winner. That name was then sealed in an envelope and placed in the vault. After the race, Sam would open the sealed envelope to show which name Jim had picked. He chose the winner every time.

The winning horses that Jim picked were: Bold Venture in 1936, Omaha in 1935, Cavalcade in 1934, Brokers Tip in 1933, Burgoo King in 1932, Twenty Grand in 1931, and Gallant Fox in 1930.

Sam was never interested in making money from Jim's abilities; he simply wanted people to know what Jim could do.

Did Jim predict only horse races, dog races, ball games, and elections? No.

One cold winter day, J. Wilbur Cook picked a kitten up out of the snow and took it to the Ruff Hotel. The following summer the cat, now named Flossie, was due to have kittens. Mr. Cook and Sam took a piece of paper and tore it into several pieces. Sam then asked Jim to pull out as many pieces of paper as Flossie would have kittens. Jim pulled out five.

Next, they wrote the word male on five pieces of paper, and the word female on another five pieces of paper. Jim was asked how many male kittens Flossie would have, and how many female kittens she would have. Jim chose three males and two females.

A week later Flossie had her kittens. Jim was correct.

Dorothy Marshall related a story about one of Jim's predictions. Her brother's wife, Eleanor, was having a baby. Dorothy's aunt Jessie held a piece of paper with "boy" written on it. Her uncle Sam held a piece of paper with "girl" written on it. Sam asked Jim to choose which gender the baby would be. Remember, there was no ultrasound then, and no one ever knew whether the baby was a boy or a girl until it was born. Jim picked "boy." Everyone eagerly awaited the birth of the child to see whether Jim had chosen correctly or not. He did.

Years later Pearl Van Arsdale recalled that Jim seemed to know her thoughts and intentions. When she would decide to leave a room Jim would go ahead of her. He always went in the right direction and into the correct room without Pearl ever saying where she was going.

CHAPTER 9 – 1937

A Sad Day

Jim Remembered

It was nice Spring weather that Thursday morning, March 18, 1937. Jim seemed to be in fairly good health and happily accompanied Sam when he left to go fishing. They drove south to Warsaw, Missouri. Sam found a good fishing spot and parked the car. Jim got out of the car, ran around and then on ahead. He abruptly lay down.

Sam called; Jim slowly got up, staggered back towards the car and collapsed. Sam scooped him up, gently placed Jim in the car, and immediately headed for Dr. Gouge's office in Sedalia. Sam stopped to phone Dr. Gouge on the way. The 35 mile drive to the vet's office in Sedalia must have seemed like it took a long time.

Dr. Gouge was ready when Sam carried Jim in.

Newspaper reports differ as to whether Jim died as Sam carried him in, or whether Jim died as he was placed on the table. The newspapers all agree, though, that his death was due to a heart attack.

Sam was heartbroken.

Pearl sent a telegram to Dorothy Marshall that read: "JIM DIED 1 OCLOCK TODAY. SAM'S GRIEF TERRIBLE."

Sam tried his best to have the dog buried in his family plot in Ridge Park Cemetery in Marshall. It was not allowed. The board of directors of the cemetery said that the cemetery was for people, not dogs. They might have also worried that letting Jim be buried there would set a precedent and they might be forced to then let other pets be buried there, also.

Pat Hays, who was sextant at Ridge Park Cemetery, in charge of maintaining the grounds, was quoted by the St. Louis Post Dispatch, and later by Outdoor Life Magazine, as saying that he didn't see what all the fuss was about "since Jim was smarter than most people in here, anyhow."

Sam arranged to have Jim buried just outside

the cemetery gates. The casket was made specially for Jim. White cloth covered the outside, and inside it was lined with white satin. A quiet, non-public funeral took place at 10 o'clock Saturday morning with a few friends and family members there.

The cemetery has since expanded; and while Jim is not in the family plot, he is now inside the cemetery with them.

The Sedalia Weekly Democrat of March 26, 1937, reported that flowers sent by Jim's admirers covered the grave. It also stated that Sam received more than 500 messages of condolence. Letters and telegrams came from all over the world from people who had known Jim or had heard of him.

According to The Saline County Citizen of March 25, 1937, the most treasured message the Van Arsdales received was a letter signed "A Lover of Dogs." It read in part: "... if there is a heaven for dogs I am sure that he is resting there."

In the years and decades since Jim lived and traveled with Sam and Pearl Van Arsdale, he has definitely not been forgotten. Many newspaper articles were written over the years, all recounting his amazing feats, all unable to explain how Jim was able to do what he did. And every so often a feature article about Jim appeared in another magazine.

Clarence Dewey Mitchell, a salesman for the Iroquois Textbook publishing company, heard about

Jim. He became so intrigued that he wrote a book titled JIM THE WONDER DOG, which was published by Dorrance and Company of Philadelphia, in 1942. Mitchell wrote the book as if Jim were telling the story. His information came from letters and comments of people who had known Jim.

On March 28, 1990, *Ripley's Believe It or Not* published a newspaper cartoon that included Jim.

Jim the Wonder Dog Memorial Garden opened in Marshall, Missouri, on May 1, 1999. A museum dedicated to Jim is next to the garden. An event called Wonder Dog Day is celebrated in Marshall each May.

And, on Thursday, June 22, 2017, Senate Bill 376 was signed by Governor Greitens designating Jim the Wonder Dog as Missouri's state wonder dog. It's official!

As Evelyn Counts of Marshall said, "He was Sam Van Arsdale's dog, but by the time he died, Jim belonged to the world."

How Did Jim Do It?

There are several theories.

One is that Sam gave some kind of signal to Jim. Many people spent a lot of time carefully watching to figure out when and how Sam told Jim what to do. Nobody detected a signal of any kind. And what kind of signal could Sam have given when Jim dashed out the door and down the street to pick out a specific car correctly?

Another theory is that of reincarnation. This theory of living more than once is usually associated with a person having a past life. There are documented cases that seem to agree with this. But nothing has been documented about reincarnation of a person to a dog. Possibly no one has thought of that…except for a group of people who said that Jim must be a reincarnation of King Solomon. Why King Solomon?

A third theory is that of mind reading. Was Jim able to see into Sam's mind, and thereby know what he was thinking? That might depend on whether people think in pictures or words. Or a combination of both.

Apparently visual thinking is fairly common in a good percentage of the population. However the number who think visually almost exclusively is much smaller. Thinking about it, though...babies are not born using words. The spoken language is something they must learn in order to better communicate. So it is quite possible that we do not think in words alone.

A Harvard study led by Elinor Armit found that people create visual images to go along with their verbal thoughts. Not only that, but people create those visual images whether they intend to or not.

So if people do visualize their thoughts, and if Jim could somehow then see those visualizations, that could explain how Jim was able to follow commands or requests when they were spoken in a foreign language. It would mean that Jim was able to read everybody's mind, though. He just did not do what anyone thought unless Sam told him to.

But if there are some people who think only in words? That might mean that Jim could actually read; not only read, but also understand many different languages.

Remember, though, when Sam asked Jim who among a group of traveling salesmen had the most change in his pocket? Nobody knew the answer, so nobody could think or visualize the answer. The men all had to fish the change out of their pockets and count it. Meanwhile, Jim was already sitting in front of the correct one.

And then there are Jim's predictions. When his prediction was sealed in an envelope, placed in a safe, and revealed at a later date, it could have been done as a magic trick. Maybe… if Sam knew how to misdirect people's attention away from the needed action. It would also include having a talent for holding and manipulating pieces of paper with your fingers in a way not visible to your audience. It is doubtful that Sam had this ability.

Even if Sam had been able to do that magic trick, it does not explain the other predictions Jim made. Flossie's kittens, or the Hunt children betting on the racetrack winners, for example.

Hardin E. Gouge, one of the veterinarians at G & G vet hospital in Sedalia, said it best. "We have seen Jim perform many times and in our opinion it was phenomenal. There was no trick and it would be impossible for anyone to train a dog to Jim's accomplishments. The only explanation that we can give is that this dog had an extra sense."

ESP?

One final thought: Why did nobody ask Jim? Probably because they were so focused on what he did, they never thought to ask him directly. But then, they would have had to write down possible answers for him to choose from—hopefully including the correct one.

We are still left without a definitive answer.

The truth is that Jim was an amazing, unexplainable, Wonder Dog.

QUESTIONS

Did Jim Have Any Puppies?
Yes

In 1931 Jim became the father of one puppy. Sam named that puppy Whoopee. It seems as though he was hoping that…maybe…this puppy, who was marked like Jim…just might have inherited some of Jim's special abilities.

Whoopee became an excellent hunting dog. But no special abilities ever came to light.

In 1933 Jim fathered two puppies. They were named Buddy and Sonny. Again they proved to be excellent hunting dogs, but neither one exhibited any of Jim's unusual abilities.

In 1935 Jim fathered two more puppies, making a total of five. These two, both females, were named Jessie and Jane. Once again, while excellent hunting dogs, neither Jessie nor Jane had any of their father's unique abilities.

Did Sam and Pearl Van Arsdale Stay in Marshall after Jim's Death?
Well…

It seems as though they never stayed put anywhere very long,, but they did leave and return to Marshall, although they continued to travel and visit relatives elsewhere.

When Sam retired, they moved to forty acres they owned on the Lake of the Ozarks. That became "home base" for them, and they named their land Jim's Point.

In 1955 when it was advertised for sale it was still known as Jim's Point.

PHOTOS

Jim with Pearl Van Arsdale; location unknown.

Jim with Sam Van Arsdale; taken on the beach.

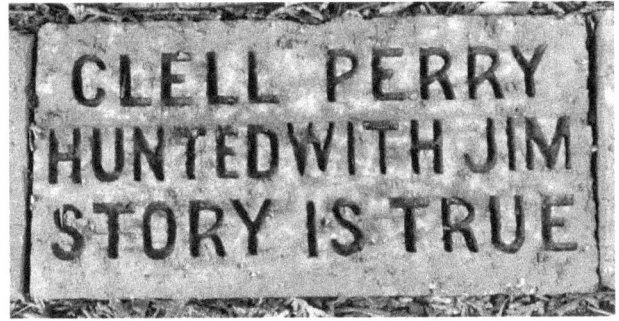

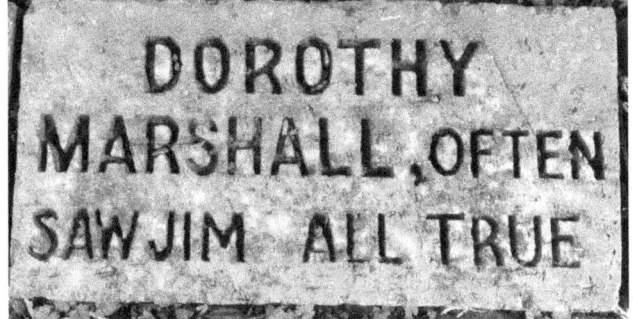

These bricks are part of the walkway in Jim the Wonder Dog Memorial Park, Marshall, MO.

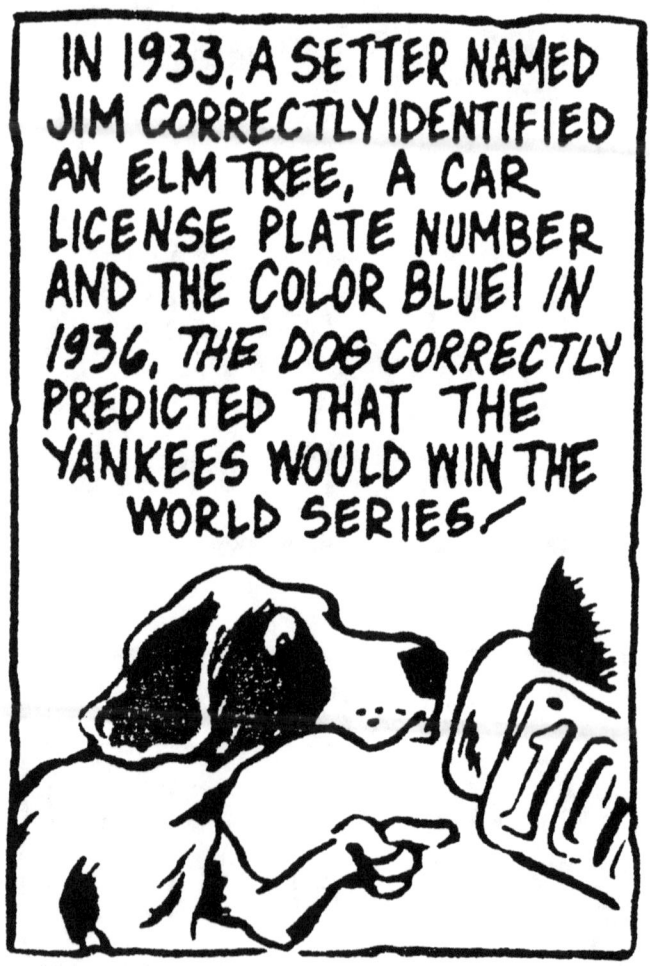

Ripley's Believe it or not cartoon from 1990.

JIM a.k.a. THE WONDER DOG

Jim's Headstone.

Jim The Wonder Dog Statue Marshal Missouri.
(Jim was given a red scarf for the winter.)

This wall hanging is in the Wonder Dog museum in Marshall. Done from Pearl's painted portrait of Jim.

SOURCES

CHAPTER 1

Unexpected delivery: reports differ, but all agree Jim was sent to Sam Van Arsdale by a traveling salesman named Taylor.
- JIM THE WONDER DOG by Clarence Dewey Mitchell (1942) p. 29-30
- *Outdoor Life*, August 1985, article Jim, The Wonder Dog by Larry Mueller
- St. Louis Post-Dispatch, Sunday Magazine, March 9, 1986, Remembering the Wonder Dog

With Dorothy
- JIM THE WONDER DOG by Clarence Dewey Mitchell (1942) p. 30-35
- *Outdoor Life*, August 1985, article Jim, The Wonder Dog by Larry Mueller

Jim gets a name
- JIM THE WONDER DOG by Clarence Dewey Mitchell (1942) p. 33-34
- *Outdoor Life*, August 1985, article Jim, The Wonder Dog by Larry Mueller

CHAPTER 2

Training
- JIM THE WONDER DOG by Clarence Dewey Mitchell (1942) p. 38-39
- www.ruralmissouri.coop, May 2014, A dog named Jim by Jim McCarty
- St. Louis Post-Dispatch, Sunday Magazine, March 9, 1986, Remembering the Wonder Dog

Ira and Sam hunt with Jim
- JIM THE WONDER DOG by Clarence Dewey Mitchell (1942) p. 41-45
- *Outdoor Life*, August 1985, article Jim, The Wonder Dog by Larry Mueller
- Various newspaper accounts have same basic information with slight differences

Number of quail
- outdoorhub.com/stories/2012/03/19/remembering, Remembering the Greatest Hunting "Wonder Dog" That Ever Lived, 75 Years After His Death

CHAPTER 3

Dance Hall explosion
- howell.mogenweb.org/article/wp_dancehallexplosion.htm has a newspaper article from Syracuse Herald, New York, dated April 4, 1928
- Https://www.gendisasters.com/missouriWestPlains,MODanceHallExplosion..., April 1928

Recognizing various trees
- JIM THE WONDER DOG by Clarence Dewey Mitchell (1942) p. 54-58
- *Outdoor Life*, August 1985, article Jim, The Wonder Dog by Larry Mueller
- St. Louis Post-Dispatch, Sunday Magazine, March 9, 1986, Remembering the Wonder Dog
- St. Cloud Times (St. Cloud, MN) December 30, 1954, p. 4 The Other Editor Says

Friends reactions
- JIM THE WONDER DOG by Clarence Dewey Mitchell (1942) p. 58-60

Dining room
- JIM THE WONDER DOG by Clarence Dewey Mitchell (1942) p. 62-63

- The Sedalia Democrat, September 13, 1931, p. 3, Dog of S. H. Van Arsdale Marvel

Warsaw, French language, and Bible
- www.ruralmissouri.org/2010Pages/10MarchJimWonderDog.html article Jim The Wonder Dog by Henry N. Ferguson

Chancellor cigars
- JIM THE WONDER DOG by Clarence Dewey Mitchell (1942) p. 66

Minnesota fishing, and frogs
- JIM THE WONDER DOG by Clarence Dewey Mitchell (1942) p. 102
- Sikeston Standard, December 11, 1931, p. 8, Dog With High School Education Photographed By Paramount Last Week Is Visiting In Sikeston

CHAPTER 4

<u>Jim goes to MU</u>
- JIM THE WONDER DOG by Clarence Dewey Mitchell (1942) p. 94-96
- Sikeston Standard, December 11, 1931, p. 8, Dog With High School Education Photographed By Paramount Last Week Is Visiting In Sikeston
- The Sedalia Democrat, December 3, 1931, p. 1, INTELLIGENCE TEST FOR "WONDER DOG"
- The Sedalia Democrat, December 6, 1931, p. 14, 'Jim" Crashes The Movies in Making Intelligence Test
- www.ruralmissouri.org/2010Pages/10MarchJimWonderDog.html article Jim The Wonder Dog by Henry N. Ferguson

<u>News feature not made</u>
- LaPlata Home Press, October 6, 1932, p. 3, "Jim" Most Wonderful Dog In America
- Wausau Daily Herald (Wausau, Wisconsin), March 4, 1932, p. 11, WHAT DO YOU WANT TO KNOW? JUST ASK "JIM"; DOG CAN PICK OUT KIND OF CARS AND TREES

Hollywood offer, dog food commercials turned down
- JIM THE WONDER DOG by Clarence Dewey Mitchell (1942) p. 109
- The Current Local (Van Buren, MO), May 27, 1971, p. 9, Jim The Wonder Dog Featured in Magazine
- *Outdoor Life*, August 1985, article Jim, The Wonder Dog by Larry Mueller

Jim's food
- *Outdoor Life*, August 1985, article Jim, The Wonder Dog by Larry Mueller

CHAPTER 5

Tied flies
- JIM THE WONDER DOG by Clarence Dewey Mitchell (1942) p. 67-68

Kemper Military Academy
- JIM THE WONDER DOG by Clarence Dewey Mitchell (1942) p. 75

Gas station
- DVD Jim The Wonder Dog © 1997 Marshall Chamber of Commerce and Missouri Valley College

H-O-F-F-M-A-N's Hardware
- JIM THE WONDER DOG by Clarence Dewey Mitchell (1942) p. 68-69
- Kansas City Times, January 26, 1932, p. 6, Dog Obeys Any Order Spoken Or Written By Its Master

Walking down Ohio Street
- Kansas City Times, January 26, 1932, p. 6, Dog Obeys Any Order Spoken Or Written By Its Master

Picture of pups
- JIM THE WONDER DOG by Clarence Dewey Mitchell (1942) p. 116-117
- *Outdoor Life*, August 1985, article Jim, The Wonder Dog by Larry Mueller

Charles M. Howell
- The Sedalia Democrat, July 20, 1932, p. 4, WONDER DOG PICKS HOWELL AS WINNER

Invitation to World's Fair
- JIM THE WONDER DOG by Clarence Dewey Mitchell (1942) p. 99
- The Sedalia Democrat, May 22, 1932, p. 3, "WONDER DOG" TO BE AT WORLD'S FAIR
- Sikeston Standard, September 30, 1932, p. 2 (no headline)
- Sikeston Standard, December 13, 1932, p. 1, JIM THE WONDER DOG MAKES BELIEVERS OUT OF CHAMBER OF COMMERCE COMMITTEE

Jim's last day hunting
- JIM THE WONDER DOG by Clarence Dewey Mitchell (1942) p. 118-129

Dr. Gouge
- JIM THE WONDER DOG by Clarence Dewey Mitchell (1942) p. 131

Dr. Flynn, treatment, operation
- JIM THE WONDER DOG by Clarence Dewey Mitchell (1942) p. 131-134
- St. Cloud Times (MN), December 30, 1954, p. 4, column: The Other Editor Says—JIM, THE WONDER DOG (from the Fergus Falls Journal)
- The Sedalia Democrat, January 8, 1933, p. 3, AN OPERATION FOR VAN ARSDALE DOG
- Sikeston Standard, August 29, 1933, p. 3, JIM IS UNSPOILED BY SPREAD OF FAME

CHAPTER 6

Sikeston Chamber of Commerce
- Sikeston Standard, December 13, 1932, p. 1, JIM THE WONDER DOG MAKES BELIEVERS OUT OF CHAMBER OF COMMERCE COMMITTEE
- JIM THE WONDER DOG by Clarence Dewey Mitchell (1942) P. 76-78

In Florida for the winter
- Sikeston Standard, April 7, 1933, p. 1, JIM HIMSELF ARRIVES FOR VISIT IN CITY
- Sikeston Standard, April 7, 1933 p. 9 JIM THE WONDER DOG MAKES A HIT WITH THE FOLKS IN TAMPA, FLA.

Miami racetrack, Hunt children
- DVD Jim The Wonder Dog © 1997 Marshall Chamber of Commerce and Missouri Valley College
- JIM THE WONDER DOG by Clarence Dewey Mitchell (1942) p. 106
- *Outdoor Life*, August 1985, article Jim, The Wonder Dog by Larry Mueller

With the Gillespie Family
- The Tampa Tribune, February 19, 1933, p.23, column Tampa Tattle by Lotta Chatter

No gambling
- The Tampa Tribune, February 25, 1933, p. 11, PICKS NO NUMBERS

More requests
- The Sedalia Democrat, May 7, 1933, p. 12, REQUEST FOR RACING TIP NOT GRANTED

CHAPTER 7

<u>In Sikeston</u>
- Sikeston Standard, April 7, 1933, p. 1, JIM, HIMSELF, ARRIVES FOR VISIT IN CITY

<u>Not at World's Fair</u>
- Sikeston Standard, May 26, 1933, p. 2, JIM, THE WONDER DOG, MAY NOT ATTEND FAIR AT CHICAGO, RHEUMATIC

<u>Fish, Game, and Forest League</u>
- Stanberry Headlight (Stanberry, MO), February 1, 1934, p. 4, part of a column: Missouri Game & Fish News by E. L. Preston

<u>Jim stays in hotels</u>
- JIM THE WONDER DOG by Clarence Dewey Mitchell (1942) p. 65

<u>In Moberly</u>
- Moberly Monitor-Index, February 14, 1935, p. 6 Sedalia "Wonder Dog" Amazes Spectators Here With Feats That Border On Miraculous

<u>At the Missouri Legislature</u>
- The Sedalia Democrat, April 25, 1935, p. 2, "JIM" BEFORE THE LEGISLATURE

- The Daily Democrat News (Marshall, MO), April 24, 1935, p. 1, "JIM" TO LEGISLATURE Van Arsdale Dog to Perform Before a Joint Session

Visit to West Plains
- St. Louis Post-Dispatch, March 19, 1937, p. 11D, JIM, 'WONDER DOG' OF SEDALIA, DIES

Fish hound
- Sedalia Weekly Democrat, October 19, 1934, p. 6, STORY ON CATCH MADE BY J.W. STOVER

Kemmerer, Wyoming
- The Kemmerer, Wyoming, Gazette, August 30, 1935, p. 8, Wonder Dog Was Here Wednesday

Listing of newspapers with "wonder dog" before Kemmerer claim
- The Sedalia Democrat, December 3, 1931, p. 1, INTELLIGENCE TEST FOR "WONDER DOG"
- The Sedalia Democrat, February 29, 1932 p. 5, ARTICLE ON "JIM" IN LONG BEACH PAPER (picture in Long Beach Press-Telegraph)

- The Sedalia Democrat, May 22, 1932, p. 3, "WONDER DOG" TO BE AT WORLD'S FAIR
- The Sedalia Democrat, July 20, 1932, p. 4, WONDER DOG PICKS HOWELL AS WINNER
- Sikeston Standard, December 13, 1932, p. 1, JIM THE WONDER DOG MAKES BELIEVERS OUT OF CHAMBER OF COMMERCE COMMITTEE
- The Tampa Tribune (Tampa, FL), February 25, 1933, p. 11, PICKS NO NUMBERS (owner of Jim, the wonder dog)
- The Sedalia Democrat, March 3, 1933, p. 15, PICTURE OF SEDALIA DOG IN TAMPA, FLA., PAPER (excellent picture of "Jim," the wonder dog)
- Sikeston Standard, April 7, 1933, p. 9, JIM THE WONDER DOG MAKES A HIT WITH THE FOLKS IN TAMPA, FLA.
- Sikeston Standard, May 26, 1933, p. 2, JIM, THE WONDER DOG, MAY NOT ATTEND FAIR AT CHICAGO, RHEUMATIC
- Sikeston Standard, August 29, 1933, p. 3, JIM IS UNSPOILED BY SPREAD OF FAME (Jim, the wonder dog is still…)
- The Sedalia Democrat, April 25, 1935, p. 2, "JIM" BEFORE THE LEGISLATURE (Jim the "wonder dog" of…)

CHAPTER 8

Move to Marshall
- https://ruralmissouri.smugmug.com/Jim-the-Wonder-Dog. Newspaper article from Jim McCarty with the headline: The Memories of Jim The Wonder Dog of the Age, Will Long Live in Marshall
- In an email from Mary Bays, Administrative Assistant of the Marshall Public Library the following was given: 1925 in West Plains; 1930 in Hotel LaMoore, Sedalia; according to Marshall Democrat News, February 1932 ,Sam managing the Ruff Hotel, renovated it and then sold it; 1935 back in Sedalia; 1936 sold the Hotel LaMoore and moved back to Marshall

Mary Pemberton
- DVD Jim The Wonder Dog © 1997 Marshall Chamber of Commerce and Missouri Valley College
- St. Louis Post-Dispatch, Sunday Magazine, March 9, 1986

John Adams
- DVD Jim The Wonder Dog © 1997 Marshall Chamber of Commerce and Missouri Valley College

- *Outdoor Life*, August 1985, article Jim, The Wonder Dog by Larry Mueller

Harold Lickey
- DVD Jim The Wonder Dog © 1997 Marshall Chamber of Commerce and Missouri Valley College
- St. Louis Post-Dispatch, Sunday Magazine, March 9, 1986

Mary Burge
- DVD Jim The Wonder Dog © 1997 Marshall Chamber of Commerce and Missouri Valley College
- www.ruralmissouri.coop, May 2014, A dog named Jim by Jim McCarty

Posing for portrait
- DVD Jim The Wonder Dog © 1997 Marshall Chamber of Commerce and Missouri Valley College
- JIM THE WONDER DOG by Clarence Dewey Mitchell (1942) p. 71

Helps in hotel
- The Daily Standard (Sikeston), June 12, 1909, p. 11, Recall Many Feats of 'Jim, the Wonder Dog'

Roy Reade
- DVD Jim The Wonder Dog © 1997 Marshall Chamber of Commerce and Missouri Valley College
- St. Louis Post-Dispatch, Sunday Magazine, March 9, 1986

Jack C. Taylor
- The Whitewright Sun (Whitewright, Texas), October 6, 1932, p. 6, INCREDIBLE, BUT VOUCHED FOR

Birdie Lee McAlister
- DVD Jim The Wonder Dog © 1997 Marshall Chamber of Commerce and Missouri Valley College
- JIM THE WONDER DOG by Clarence Dewey Mitchell (1942) p. 72-73
- *Outdoor Life*, August 1985, article Jim, The Wonder Dog by Larry Mueller

John Adams
- DVD Jim The Wonder Dog © 1997 Marshall Chamber of Commerce and Missouri Valley College

Charles Fitzgerald
- DVD Jim The Wonder Dog © 1997 Marshall Chamber of Commerce and Missouri Valley College

Charles Bradford
- DVD Jim The Wonder Dog © 1997 Marshall Chamber of Commerce and Missouri Valley College

Billy Ray Moore
- DVD Jim The Wonder Dog © 1997 Marshall Chamber of Commerce and Missouri Valley College

Jim Gabb
- DVD Jim The Wonder Dog © 1997 Marshall Chamber of Commerce and Missouri Valley College

Della Mae Soloman
- DVD Jim The Wonder Dog © 1997 Marshall Chamber of Commerce and Missouri Valley College

Earl Shannon
- DVD Jim The Wonder Dog © 1997 Marshall Chamber of Commerce and Missouri Valley College

Dorothy Marshall
- DVD Jim The Wonder Dog © 1997 Marshall Chamber of Commerce and Missouri Valley College

Pearl Van Arsdale
- The Desert Sun (Palm Springs, California), November 22, 1955, p. 10, Dog with Occult Powers Still Remembered in Ozarks

Yankees win world series
- St. Louis Post-Dispatch, Sunday Magazine, March 9, 1986
- JIM THE WONDER DOG by Clarence Dewey Mitchell (1942) p. 104

Roosevelt's presidential win
- JIM THE WONDER DOG by Clarence Dewey Mitchell (1942) p. 105-106

Kentucky Derby Winners
- St. Louis Post-Dispatch, Sunday Magazine, March 9, 1986
- JIM THE WONDER DOG by Clarence Dewey Mitchell (1942) p. 108

Flossie and her kittens
- St. Louis Post-Dispatch, Sunday Magazine, March 9, 1986

- JIM THE WONDER DOG by Clarence Dewey Mitchell (1942)
- *Outdoor Life*, August 1985, article Jim, The Wonder Dog by Larry Mueller

CHAPTER 9

Jim's Death
- Sedalia Weekly Democrat, March 19, 1937, p. 3, JIM THE WONDER DOG DIES AFTER A HEART ATTACK
- Moberly Monitor-Index, March 19, 1937, p. 2, MARSHALL MAN'S WONDER DOG DOES
- Marshall Democrat, March 20, 1937, p. 1, FAMOUS DOG BURIED HERE TODAY
- St. Louis Post-Dispatch, March 19, 1937, p. 11D, JIM 'WONDER DOG' OF SEDALIA DIES
- Democrat-News (Marshall, MO), March 18, 1937, p. 1, WONDER DOG, JIM, DEAD FROM HEART ATTACK

Pearl's telegram to Dorothy
- *Outdoor Life*, August 1985, article Jim, The Wonder Dog by Larry Mueller

Ridge Park Cemetery refusal
- www.ruralmissouri.coop, May 2014, A dog named Jim by Jim McCarty
- www.ruralmissouri.org/2010Pages/10MarchJimWonderDog.html article Jim The Wonder Dog by Henry N. Ferguson

Casket
- The Saline County Citizen (Marshall, MO), March 25, 1937, JIM BURIED IN SPECIAL CASKET HERE SATURDAY
- Sedalia Weekly Democrat, March 26, 1937, p. 3, SPECIAL CASKET FOR "WONDER DOG"

Mitchell's book about Jim
- https://douglascountyhearld.com/2017/07/the-snoop column "The Snoop" by Keith Moore
- The Sikeston Herald, June 4, 1942, p 4, BOOK ON LIFE OF "JIM, THE WONDER DOG"
- JIM THE WONDER DOG by Clarence Dewey Mitchell © 1942

Missouri State Wonder Dog
- https://legiscan.com/MO/text/SB376/2017. (amends chapter 10, RSMo, by adding two new sections, one of which is Sect. A 10.113 designating Jim as Missouri's Wonder Dog
- http://www.marshallnews.com/story/2422414.html The Marshall Democrat-News, June 22, 2017, Jim the Wonder Dog named Missouri's Wonder Dog

Quote from Evelyn Counts
- DVD Jim The Wonder Dog © 1997 Marshall Chamber of Commerce and Missouri Valley College

HOW DID JIM DO IT?

Elinor Armit
- https://news.harvard.edu/gazette/story/2017/05/visual-images-often-i…

Hardin E. Gouge, D.V.M.
- Reissue of Jim the Wonder Dog ©1942 by C. D. Mitchell and ©1970 by H. J. Hausam "This copyright expires December 31, 2017 by right of the Copyright Act of 1976 - U.S.A." published Sedalia, MO, 1989. On back cover.

QUESTIONS
Jim's puppies
- Saline County Citizen (Marshall, Missouri), March 25, 1937, p. 7, JIM BURIED IN SPECIAL CASKET HERE SATURDAY

Jim's Point
- The Sedalia Democrat, May 23, 1955, p. 8, 86—Shore, Mountain, Lake for Sale

ABOUT THE AUTHOR

Nancy Dailey
(Photo by Bob Linder}

Nancy Dailey lived a year in Germany as a teenager, where she learned the language, At the University of Missouri she majored in art.

After more than 30 years teaching in Missouri classrooms, Nancy set out on new adventures: geocaching, zip-lining, writing, and traveling-- especially for research.

Nancy continues to try new ideas and things. Who has time to sit in a rocking chair when there is so much out there to see and do? So, while Nancy lives in Springfield, Missouri, there is no telling where you will find her. Or what she will be doing.

For more information about Nancy, her writing, artwork, etc. please visit her website:
www.nancy-dailey.com

Notes

Notes

www.ingramcontent.com/pod-product-compliance
Lightning Source LLC
Chambersburg PA
CBHW060847050426
42453CB00008B/865